This
Book
Belongs
To _

Grolier Enterprises Inc.
SHERMAN TURNPIKE, DANBURY, CONNECTICUT 06816

Book Club Edition

An **ALICE** IN **BIBLELAND** ® Storybook

The STORY Of BABY MOSES

Written by Alice Joyce Davidson
Illustrated by Victoria Marshall

Text copyright ©1985 by Alice Joyce Davidson
Art copyright ©1985 by The C.R. Gibson Company
Published by The C.R. Gibson Company
Norwalk, Connecticut 06856
Printed in the United States of America
All rights reserved
ISBN 0-8378-5071-1
D.L. TO: 203-1988

Alice liked to read a lot.
It always made her glad
To read a Bible story
From a picture book she had.

One day she sat down by a stream,
And the story that she read
Was about a baby, Moses,
And a tiny basket bed.

As Alice sat there studying
Each picture and each word,
She got this little message
From her friend the airmail bird:
  "Reading is the magic key
  To take you where you want to be."

The book that Alice held became
A giant magic screen.
She walked on through to Bibleland
And came upon this scene.

She saw Israelites in Egypt.
They were happy living there.
As years went by the families grew.
They had good things to share.

But all this changed when one sad day
A new king took the throne.
He was the meanest pharaoh
The Israelites had ever known.

He saw the peaceful Israelites
Living on his land
And feared they'd turn against him,
So this is what he planned.

He made them slave and build for him,
He worked them day and night,
But still the pharaoh was afraid
Of every Israelite.

The wicked pharaoh made a law
To drown each new-born son
Of every Israelite family,
And this dreadful deed was done.

One mother kept in hiding
A sturdy baby boy.
The family loved him dearly
And he filled their hearts with joy.

For three long months she kept him
Hidden from the soldiers' view,
But she feared the pharaoh's soldiers
Would take her baby, too.

So the mother wove a basket,
And she sealed it like a boat,
Then she brought it to the river
To check that it would float.

She put it by the riverside
Between tall grass to hide it,
Then she rocked her baby boy to sleep
And put him down inside it.

The river gently rocked it.
Up and down the basket went,
And safe inside the basket
The baby was content.

The baby's sister hid nearby
Behind tall grass to see
What would happen to her brother
Who was as dear as he could be.

The daughter of the pharaoh
And her maids stopped by that day.
They came down to the river
To take a bath and play.

The pharaoh's daughter looked around,
And by the riverside,
She saw the little basket
Where the baby slept inside.

Her maids brought her the basket
With the baby Israelite.
The pharaoh's daughter touched him,
And he held her finger tight.

The pharaoh's daughter pitied him
When he began to cry.
She held him, and she rocked him
And she sang this lullaby.

"Hush, dear baby Israelite,
Hush, dear little one.
I'll save you and take care of you
As if you were my son."

Then the baby's sister
Came out of hiding, too,
And said, "I know a nursemaid
Who can be of help to you."

The pharaoh's daughter answered her,
"I'd like that very much.
This baby boy should have a nurse
Who has a tender touch."

The baby's sister ran back home
With news about her brother,
And the nursemaid she returned with
Was the baby boy's own mother!

The daughter of the pharaoh
Gladly hired her and said,
"I found this little baby
In this tiny basket bed."

"I want you to take care of him,
And when your work is done,
I'll take him back and raise him;
I'll treat him as my son."

So the mother took the basket
And her heart was filled with joy.
She was glad to act as nursemaid
To her precious baby boy.

When the boy was old enough,
His mother took him to
The daughter of the pharaoh
As she'd been told to do.

"This boy will be my own son now,"
Exclaimed the pharaoh's daughter,
"And I think I'll call him Moses
For I took him from the water."

Alice then left Bibleland,
Walked through her magic screen,
And as she did she thought about
The baby she had seen.

She knew that saving Moses
Was part of God's great plan
For Moses became a prophet
And a very holy man.

Moses led God's chosen people.
He taught them all God's way.
Moses brought the Ten Commandments
Alice follows every day!